BASIC/NOT BORING

SOCIAL STUDIES

Grades K-1

Inventive Exercises to Sharpen Skills and Raise Achievement

Series Concept & Development
by Imogene Forte & Marjorie Frank
Exercises by Charlotte Poulos

Incentive Publications, Inc.
Nashville, Tennessee

About the cover:
Bound resist, or tie dye, is the most ancient known method of
fabric surface design. The brilliance of the basic tie dye design
on this cover reflects the possibilities that emerge from the
mastery of basic skills.

Illustrated by Kathleen Bullock
Cover art by Mary Patricia Deprez, dba Tye Dye Mary®
Cover design by Marta Drayton, Joe Shibley, and W. Paul Nance
Edited by Anna Quinn

ISBN 0-86530-388-6

PRINTED IN THE UNITED STATES OF AMERICA

TABLE OF CONTENTS

Appendix

CELEBRATE BASIC SOCIAL STUDIES SKILLS

Basic does not mean boring! There is certainly nothing dull about . . .
>   . . . roaming the world to learn about new people and places
>   . . . checking out the lumps and bumps on the Earth's surface
>   . . . delivering cookies to practice reading addresses
>   . . . figuring out where you are in the universe
>   . . . tracking down famous people, birds, and houses of America
>   . . . using clever maps to find a lost cat or dog
>   . . . finding out why you should not eat squiggly worms

These are just some of the adventures students can explore as they celebrate basic social studies skills. The idea of celebrating the basics is just what it sounds like—enjoying and improving the skills that help you learn about people, their places in the world, and their activities. Each page of this book invites young learners to try a high-interest, visually appealing exercise that will sharpen one specific social studies skill or concept. This is not just an ordinary fill-in-the-blanks way to learn. These exercises are fun and surprising. Students will do the useful work of sharpening social studies skills while they follow two inquisitive children and their pets around the neighborhood, the country, and the world. Along with these fictional characters, they can learn about how people live together, grow, work, and learn.

The pages in this book can be used in many ways:
- to review or practice a skill with one student
- to sharpen the skill with a small or large group
- to begin a lesson on a particular skill
- to assess how well a student has mastered a skill

Each page has directions that are written simply. An adult should be available to help students read the information on the page, if needed.

In most cases, the pages will be used best as a follow-up to a lesson that has already been taught. The pages are excellent tools for immediate reinforcement of a skill or concept.

As your students take on the challenges of these adventures with social studies, they will grow! And as you watch them check off the basic skills they've strengthened, you can celebrate with them.

The Skills Test

Use the skills test beginning on page 58 as a pretest and/or a post-test. This will help you check the students' mastery of basic social studies skills and will prepare them for success on achievement tests.

SKILLS CHECKLIST
SOCIAL STUDIES, GRADES K-1

✔	SKILL	PAGE(S)
	Be aware of people, places, and things in the world	10, 11
	Identify characteristics of self; increase self-awareness	12, 13
	Identify ways people grow, learn, and change	14, 15
	Recognize many kinds of families	16, 17
	Identify important people in your life	16, 17, 21
	Identify roles and functions of families	18–20
	Find information on a chart	20
	Identify different skills that people have	22, 34, 35
	Identify basic needs that all people have	23
	Describe and distinguish between people's needs and wants	23–25
	Identify different kinds of shelter	26, 27
	Recognize some different social groups	28
	Identify some rules of societies or families	29
	Read addresses; know your own address	30, 31
	Find information on maps	30, 31, 38, 39, 44–47, 53, 55, 56
	Make a map of your room	32
	Identify places in neighborhoods and communities	33
	Identify people and jobs in communities	34
	Distinguish between goods and services	35
	Describe some ways money is used in a community	36
	Identify different kinds of transportation	37
	Locate places on a U.S. map	38, 39
	Locate your home on a map of the U.S. and a map of the world	38, 39, 46, 47
	Identify some U.S. symbols, traditions, places, and holidays	40, 42, 43
	Identify some famous Americans and their accomplishments	41
	Become familiar with maps of the world; locate continents	44–47
	Explore something about families or cultures throughout the world	44, 45, 51
	Identify some different landforms	48
	Become familiar with some geographic terms and concepts	49
	Explore the concept of climate	50
	Examine flags of some nations	51, 52
	Read a grid map	53
	Identify N, S, E, W directions	54
	Read information from a simple timeline	57

SOCIAL STUDIES
Grades K-1

Skills Exercises

What in the World?

What an adventure!
Layla and Jeff are off on a bike ride with their pets, Biff and Tulip.
They want to explore many places.
They will see many interesting things.
Color the things in the picture that you have seen.

Name _____

Environmental Awareness

Basic Skills/Social Studies K-1

What in the World? cont.

Color the things that you have seen.

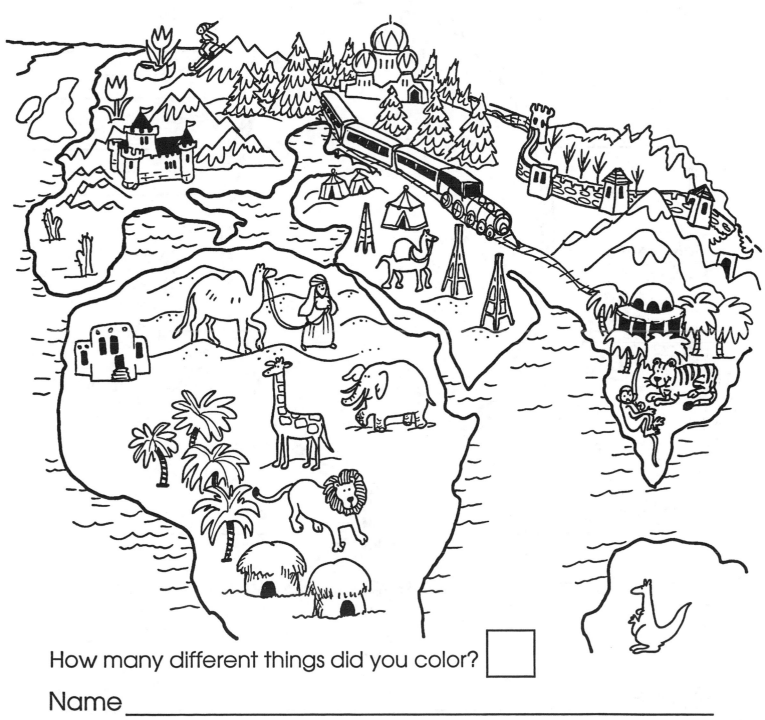

How many different things did you color?

Name

Use with page 10.

11

Basic Skills/Social Studies K-1

Environmental Awareness

Meet a VIP!

The letters VIP stand for "Very Important Person."
You are a VIP because no one in the whole world is just like you!
Draw a picture of yourself in the mirror.
Then finish the sentences to tell about you—a VIP!

I really like

I do not like

I worry about

I am good at

Name _____

Look What You Can Do!

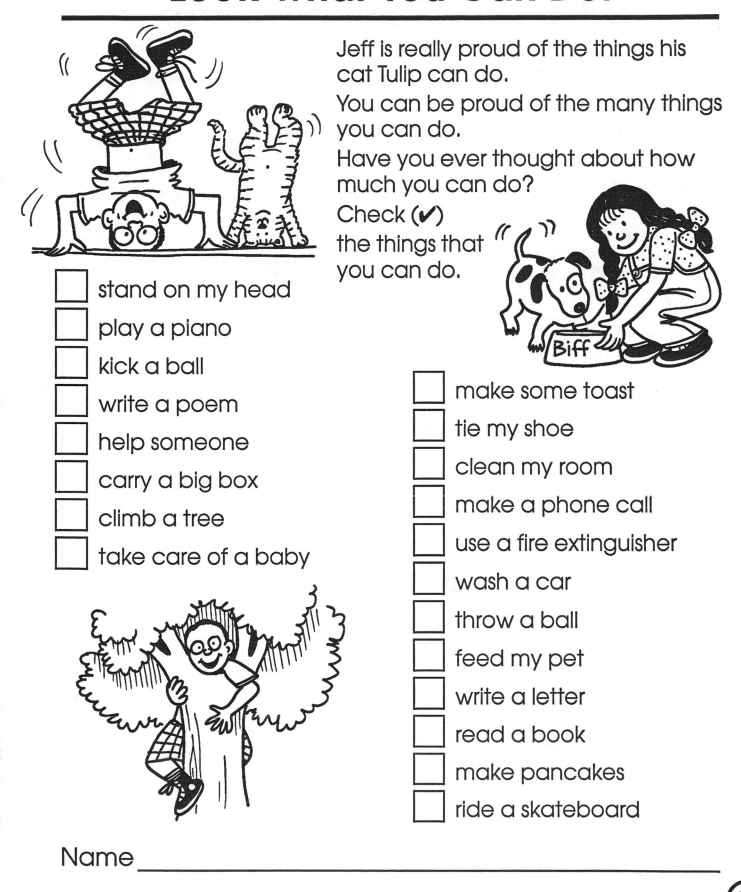

Jeff is really proud of the things his cat Tulip can do.

You can be proud of the many things you can do.

Have you ever thought about how much you can do?

Check (✔) the things that you can do.

- [ ] stand on my head
- [ ] play a piano
- [ ] kick a ball
- [ ] write a poem
- [ ] help someone
- [ ] carry a big box
- [ ] climb a tree
- [ ] take care of a baby

- [ ] make some toast
- [ ] tie my shoe
- [ ] clean my room
- [ ] make a phone call
- [ ] use a fire extinguisher
- [ ] wash a car
- [ ] throw a ball
- [ ] feed my pet
- [ ] write a letter
- [ ] read a book
- [ ] make pancakes
- [ ] ride a skateboard

Name _____

Self-Awareness

Once upon a Time

Everyone was a tiny baby once upon a time.

We don't stay babies for long because we always grow, learn, and change.

We need to look at pictures to remember how little we were!

Look at Layla's pictures, and see how she has changed.

Write the number of the picture or pictures that show:

1. Layla's dad helping her learn something ____

2. Layla teaching something to her little brother ____

3. Layla learning something as a baby ____

4. Layla learning something all by herself ____ and ____

Name _____

May be used with page 15.

Growth, Learning, & Change

Basic Skills/Social Studies K-1

Yesterday, Today, and Tomorrow

Do you dream about the things you will do when you are a big kid?

Do you remember things you did when you were a little kid?

Look at the pictures of the baby, the child, and the teenager.

Draw something to go along with each picture.

Jeff, age 1

This is something babies can do.

Jeff, age 5

This is something 5-year-olds can do.

Jeff, age 15

This is something teenagers can do.

Name _____

May be used with page 14.

Growth, Learning, & Change

All Shapes & Sizes

People come in different shapes, colors, and sizes.
Do you know what? So do families!
Each family is different and special.
Count the number of people in each different family.
Then draw a picture of your own family.

Name _____

F ☐

G ☐

H ☐

I ☐

Draw your own family here!

Name _____

Big Helping Hands

Layla's family and your family are like families all over the world.
People in families try to help each other.
What are some of the ways the big people in your family help you?
Write five ways on the big hand.
Can you write on the fingers?

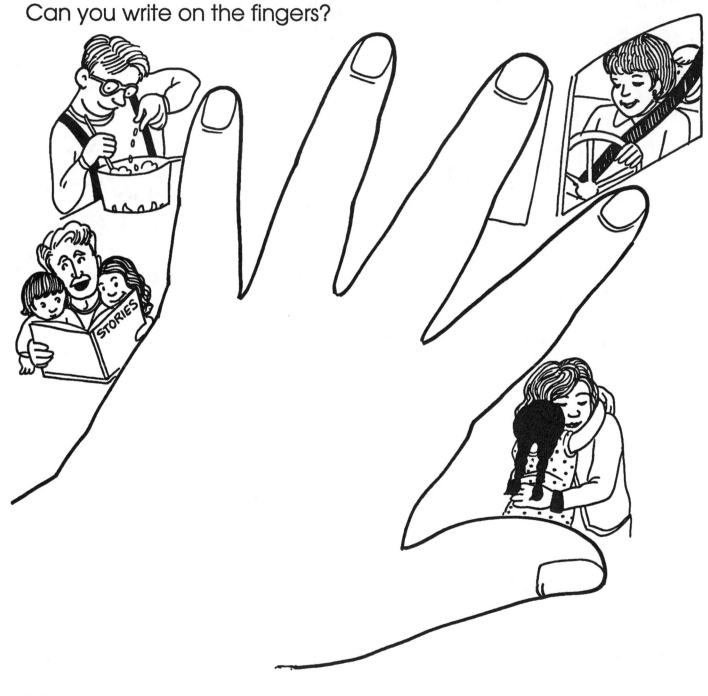

Name _____

Little Helping Hands

Small people help families, too!
Trace around your own hand on this page.
Write some things you do to help your family.
Write on the hand or fingers.

Name _____

May be used with page 18.

Basic Skills/Social Studies K-1

Roles & Functions in Families

Good Job!

It's time to clean up after Biff again!
This is one of Layla's jobs!
The stars show which jobs each family member does.

Name	Take Care of Dog	Wash Dishes	Vacuum	Clean Windows	Cook Dinner
Layla	☆			☆	
Dad			☆		☆
Mom		☆			☆
Grandma			☆	☆	

1. Color the stars for Layla's jobs blue.

2. Color the stars for Dad's jobs green.

3. Color the stars for Grandma's jobs red.

4. Color the stars for Mom's jobs purple.

5. Name a job that you do in your family.

_____

_____

_____

Name _____

It's Good to Have Friends!

Friends come in all sizes, shapes, and colors—just like families.
They can be young or old or your own age.
Friends are people you share, work, or play with.
Look for friends in this picture.

Use these colors to color the clothing on some friends:

1. GREEN—a friend who is an older person
2. YELLOW—a friend who is very young
3. PURPLE—someone who is being a friend to a small child
4. BLUE—someone who is being a friend to a pet
5. RED—someone who is helping a hurt friend

Draw a circle around someone you might like for a friend.

Name _____

Everybody Is Good at Something

Do you know someone who can play a tuba or build a boat?

People have many different skills. Everybody is good at something!

Color the picture if you know someone who can do the skill it shows.

Then answer the questions below.

Do you know someone who can . . .

. . . play a violin?

. . . build a house?

. . . fix cars?

. . . paint?

. . . cook?

. . . sing well?

. . . listen well?

. . . tell a good story?

. . . use a computer?

. . . grow a garden?

. . . ride a motorcycle?

Name _____

What Everybody Needs

Biff and Tulip are hungry. They need food!

The picture shows things that people need, too.

The words in the **Word Box** name things people need.

Draw a line from each word to the part of the picture that shows the need.

Word Box

shelter • food • air • water • clothing • love • sunshine • friends

Name _____

Do You Really Need It?

Both kids say they **need** some things.
Only some of the things are real **needs**; the other things are **wants**.
Color the bubbles that name real **needs**.

1. I need a new skateboard.

2. I need a warm coat.

3. I need food to eat.

4. I need chocolate cake.

5. I need a dollhouse for my dolls.

6. I need a place to live.

7. I need friends and family to love.

8. I need a toy robot with wings and wheels.

9. I need cartoons to watch on television.

10. I need fresh air to breathe.

11. I need exercise.

12. I need a new car.

Name _____

Needs & Wants

Basic Skills/Social Studies K-1

Making Choices

Layla and Jeff are looking at a catalog of many things to buy.
They know they can't have everything they want.
They must choose things they want the most.
Color the five things you would want the most.

If your mom or dad wanted five things,
would they be the same things that you want?
Circle five things you think your mom or dad would want.

Name _____

Home Sweet Home

All people and animals, big and small, need a place to live that keeps them safe.

Look at all the creatures and homes on this page and on page 27.

Draw a path to help each person or animal find the way home.

Name _____

Home Sweet Home, cont.

Draw a path to help each person or animal find the way home.

Name _____

Use with page 26.

Kinds of Shelter

The Growing Garden

The world is like a big garden with paths that lead to many places and groups where you can grow and learn.
The path begins in your home with your family.
It goes to other places or groups where you grow and learn.
Some of these groups and places are named in the box.
Write the number of the picture next to the matching word.

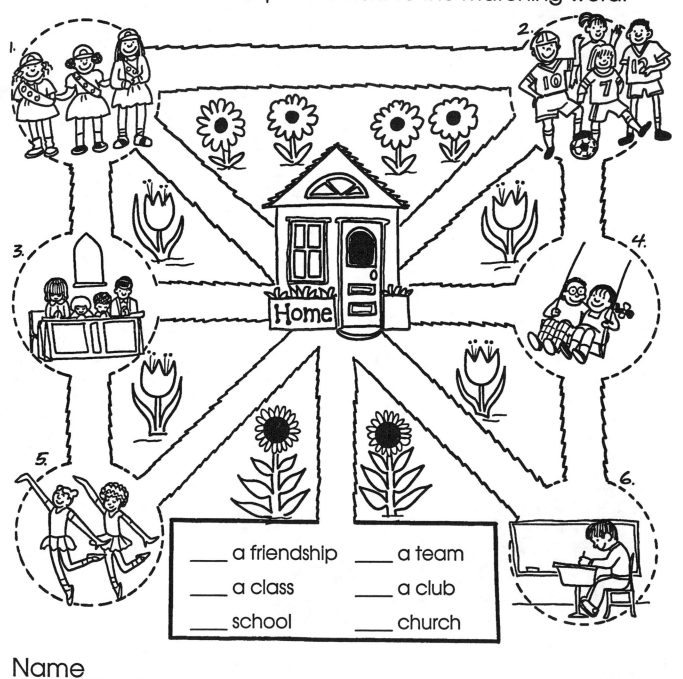

____ a friendship   ____ a team

____ a class   ____ a club

____ school   ____ church

Name _____

What Are Rules For?

Rules have reasons: they keep people safe and healthy.
They also help people get along.
Write the number of the picture that shows the answer.

1. Which picture shows a rule to keep someone healthy? ____
2. Which picture shows a rule to keep someone safe?   ____
3. Which picture shows a rule about sharing?   ____
4. Color the picture that shows someone
   not following a rule.

Name _____

Cookie Delivery

Layla is a Girl Scout.

She is delivering cookies to her neighbors.

Help her and her mom find the right addresses.

The number of a house and the name of a street make up an address.

Use the map on this page and on page 31.

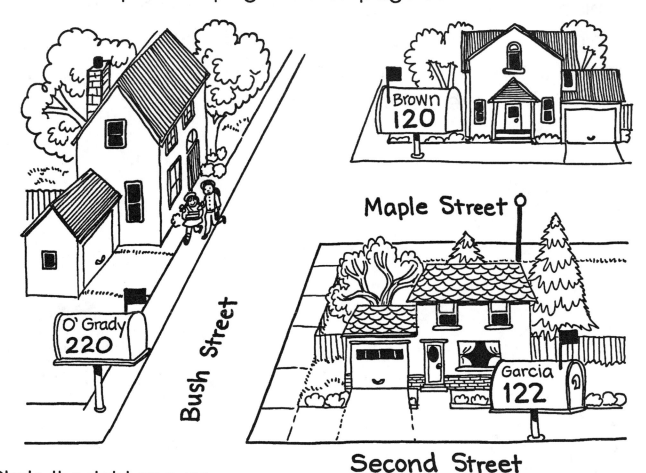

Circle the right answer.

1. Layla likes to pet the O'Gradys' cat. What is their address?

   124 Maple Street   220 Maple Street   220 Bush Street

2. Who lives at 126 Second Street?

   The Adams   The Steins   The Browns

Name _____

Use with page 31.

Read Addresses

Basic Skills/Social Studies K-1

3. Which families share a house on Second Street?

The Chens and the Adams

The Browns and the Chens   The Travises and the Habeebs

4. Who lives next door to the Garcias?

The Habeebs   The Steins   The Adams

Maple Street

Second Street

5. What street does Layla cross to get from the Browns' to the Garcias'?

Bush Street   Maple Street   Second Street

6. What is the Chens' address?

120 Maple Street   124 Second Street   124 Maple Street

Name _____

Just the Way You Want It

Layla wants to change her room around.

She is making a map of the way she wants her room to be.

Have you ever wanted to change your room?

Draw a map of your room with everything the way you want it!

Name _____

Make a Map

Where Should He Go?

When Jeff wants to read a good book, he goes to his town library.
The library is on the map in row B and row 4. It is at B, 4.
Where should Jeff go to do the things below?
Give the location on the map for each answer.
Where should he go to . . .

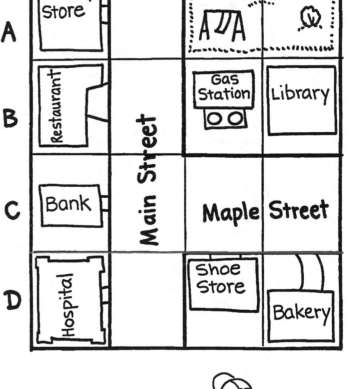

1. . . . buy groceries? **A, 1**

2. . . . save money? ____

3. . . . play on a swing? ____

4. . . . see a doctor? ____

5. . . . eat a hamburger? ____

6. . . . buy shoes? ____

7. . . . get gas? ____

8. . . . buy fresh bread? ____

Name _____

Workers Everywhere You Look!

Wow! What a busy bustling city!

On their bus ride across the city, Layla and Jeff see many people working at different jobs!

Circle as many different workers as you can find.

Color the ones who are doing something you might like to do.

How many workers did you find? _____

Name _____

Workers in the Community

Basic Skills/Social Studies K-1

Goods & Services Are Both Good!

Some workers make or grow things. These things are called **goods.**
Some workers do things for people. These things are called **services.**
Look for workers making or growing goods. Circle them with red.
Look for workers serving someone. Circle them with blue.

Color the worker who is doing a service for Jeff and Layla.

Name _____

Goods & Services

Money Can't Buy Everything

Layla has a purse full of money, and she wants to buy some things!
Even though she has a lot of money, she cannot buy everything.
Look for things that money can buy and that money cannot buy.
Color the things that money cannot buy.

Name _____

Coming and Going

Jeff and Layla get around on their bicycle.
People get around lots of other ways, too.
They can drive, float, fly, skate, sail, bike, or take a train!
Color all the kinds of transportation that you have used.
Draw a circle around your favorite kind of transportation.

Name _____

Which State Is Yours?

Name _____

Read a U.S. Map

Jeff and his family took a trip across the United States.

Can you find his family?

Use a red crayon to trace Jeff's route.

Read the names of all the states he and his family traveled through.

1. Find your state. Put a ★ to show where you live in your state. Then color your state purple.

2. Find all the states that touch your state. Color them green.

3. Find a state you would like to visit. Color it yellow.

Name _____

The American Parade

The kids are marching in a big parade to celebrate the United States.

The parade is full of American symbols.

Symbols are special pictures or things that stand for something about the country.

Look for all the symbols listed below. Color each one as you find it.

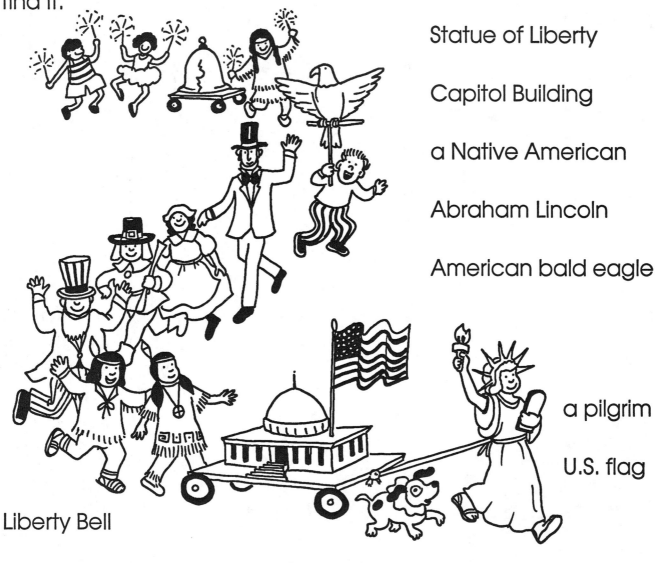

Statue of Liberty

Capitol Building

a Native American

Abraham Lincoln

American bald eagle

a pilgrim

U.S. flag

Liberty Bell

Uncle Sam

Name _____

Some Very Famous People

Jeff loves the museum.

It is full of all kinds of interesting things from the past.

Today he is looking at pictures of some important Americans.

Write the number from each picture next to the matching name.

Museum Guide

1.

2.

3.

4.

5.

Martin Luther King, Jr.
A leader who helped get fair treatment for black Americans

Abraham Lincoln
American president who helped free the slaves

Betsy Ross
Woman who probably made the first U.S. flag

Sally Ride
America's first female astronaut to travel in space

George Washington
America's first president

Name _____

Special Americans

A Very Famous Bird

The American bald eagle is a symbol for the United States.
It is the most famous bird in America!
Connect the dots to see what this eagle looks like!

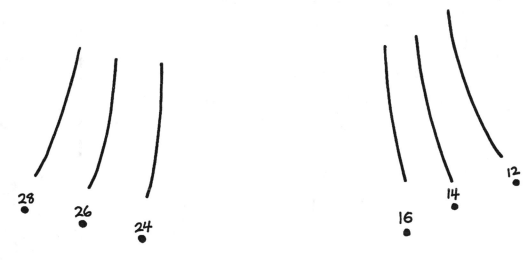
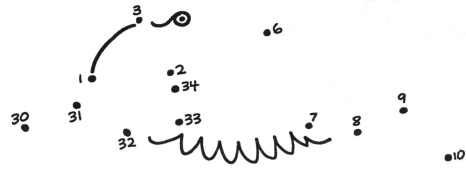
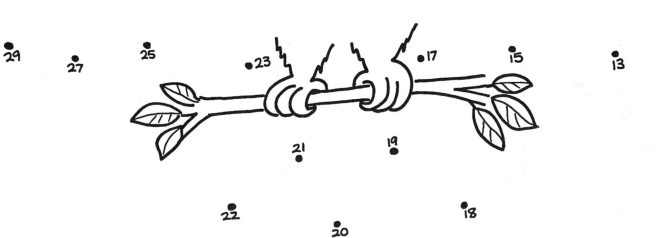

Name _____

American Symbols

A Very Famous House

It's the most famous house in the United States!
The address is 1600 Pennsylvania Avenue in Washington, DC.
Connect the dots, and you will make a picture of this great house!

This is the White House.
It has 54 rooms and 16 bathrooms.
It is the home for the president of the United States.

The president's office is in a part of the White House.

What is the president's name?

_____

_____

Name _____

Everyone Is from Somewhere!

These kids live in homes all over the world.

Which one is from which continent?

Each kid has a clue to tell you
which continent is home.

Draw a line from each kid to the
right spot for his or her home.

Layla lives in the
United States on
the continent of
North America.

Roberto is from Brazil
on the continent of
South America.

Name _____

Draw a line from each kid to the right spot for his or her home.

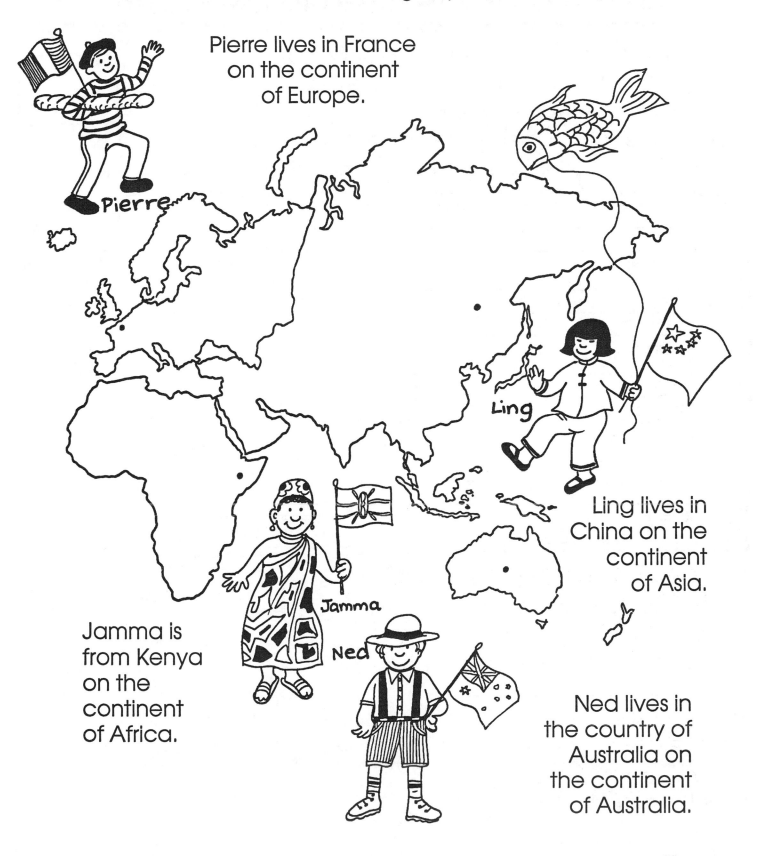

Pierre lives in France on the continent of Europe.

Pierre

Ling

Jamma

Ned

Jamma is from Kenya on the continent of Africa.

Ling lives in China on the continent of Asia.

Ned lives in the country of Australia on the continent of Australia.

Name _____

Where in the World Are You?

What if the mail carrier wants to deliver a
letter to you, but does not have your address.
Where in the world are you?
Give the mail carrier a little help in finding you.
Write your address on the mailbox, and draw your home.

Draw your home here.

Your Name

Your Street

Your City

Your State

If you live in the United States,
color your state at the right.
If not, write the name of
your state or province here.

Put a ★ to show where
your town or city is.

Name _____

Use with page 47.
Locate Home

Basic Skills/Social Studies K-1

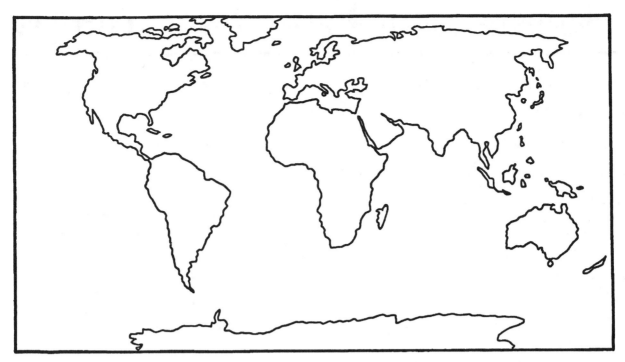

Color the continent that you live on.

Write the name of
your country here. _____

Write the name of
your continent here. _____

Find your planet. Color it.

Write the name of
your planet here. _____

Name _____

The Earth Has Bumps and Lumps

Jeff likes to draw the bumps and lumps of the land wherever he travels.

He draws a map to show different kinds of land and water.

Follow the directions to color Jeff's map.

1. Draw a 🐟 in the bay.

2. Draw a 🏠 on the peninsula.

3. Draw a ⛵ on the lake.

4. Draw some 🌸 on the plain.

5. Draw a 🌴 on the island.

6. Draw a 🚩 on a mountain.

7. Color the river blue.

Name _____

Puzzled by Geography

These good friends are doing a geography puzzle.
They are getting a little help from Tulip, the cat.
They need your help, too.

Look at the picture clues, and then find the answers in the **Word Box**.

CLUES

Down

1.
2.
3.

Across

4.
5.
6.
7.

WORD BOX

bay
island
volcano
mountain
globe
ocean
trees

Name _____

Geography Terms

Some Like It Hot! Some Like It Cold!

These four travelers are all dressed for different climates.
Help them find the right place to go.
Draw a path from each one to the climate that is the
right match!

Name _____

Climate

Many Ways to Say "Hello!"

These kids are all saying "hello" in their own languages.
They are standing on maps of their countries, and they are wearing their native dress.
They are holding flags of their countries!
Read the names of the countries, and color each flag.

Name _____

Copyright ©1998 by Incentive Publications, Inc., Nashville, TN.
Basic Skills/Social Studies K-1

Cultural Characteristics

Great Flags!

Every country has a flag!

They are all different and beautiful.

In art class, Jeff and Layla are drawing flags of some different countries around the world.

Help them color these flags from four different countries.

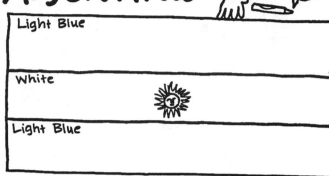

Argentina

Light Blue

White

Light Blue

Canada

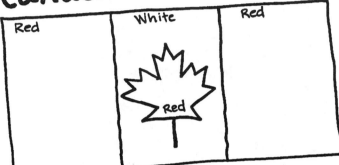

Red

White

Red

Red

Philippines

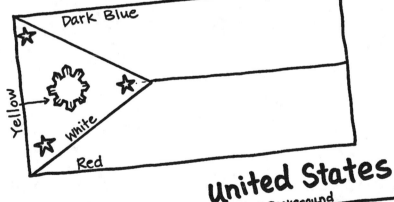

Dark Blue

Yellow

White

Red

United States

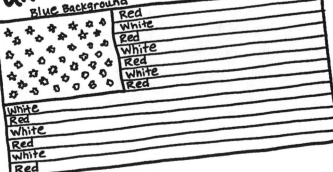

Blue Background

Red
White
Red
White
Red
White
Red

White
Red
White
Red
White
Red

Name _____

Which Square?

Two friends are taking a rest on the bench in the park.
Which square are they sitting in?
The square is in row A and row 2. They are in square A, 2!
Find some other things on the park map!

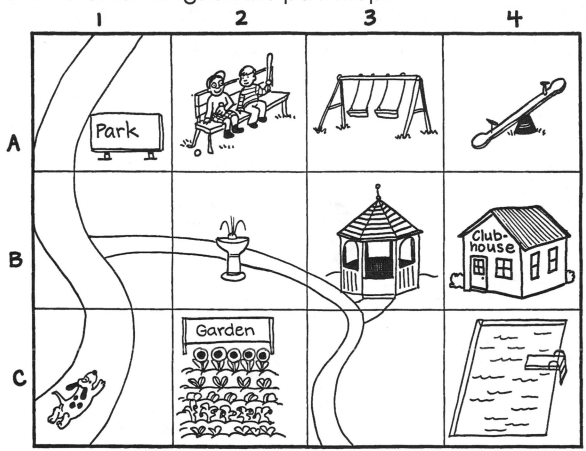

1. Where is the ? _____

2. Where is the ? _____

3. Where is the ? _____

4. Color the thing in C, 2 green.

5. Where is the  ? _____

6. Where is the ? _____

7. Where is the [Park] ? _____

8. Color the building in B, 4 red.

Name _____

Never Eat Squiggly Worms!

This silly sentence is a good one for you to remember.
It helps you remember the directions on the Earth and on maps.
The first letter of each word stands for the first letter of the direction:

N—NORTH   **E—EAST**   **S—SOUTH**   **W—WEST**

Layla is using her arms and legs to show the directions.

1. Write the correct direction in each space.
2. The sun rises in the east in the morning.
   Draw a bright yellow sun on the east side of the paper.
3. The sun sets in the west in the evening.
   Draw a beautiful red sunset on the west side of the paper.

Name _____

Where Is Tulip?

Tulip was at home with Jeff just a few minutes ago.
Now she is lost somewhere in the neighborhood!
Will Jeff find her?
Draw Jeff's trail on the map and find out!

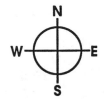

1. Jeff leaves his apartment.

2. He looks behind Sam's house.

3. He walks south on Maple Street.

4. He looks in the swimming pool.

5. He looks under the slide.

6. He looks behind the school.

7. He looks in Layla's house.

8. He looks in Maria's yard.

9. He looks in the sandbox.

10. He finds Tulip at the top of the flagpole!

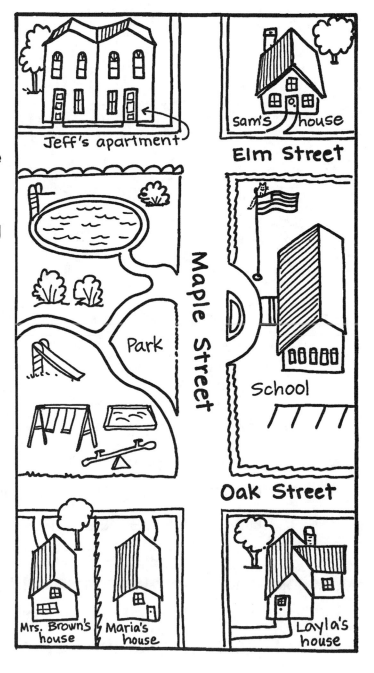

Name _____

Looking for Biff

Jeff and Layla are off on their bicycle looking for another lost pet!
Follow the paw prints with Jeff and Layla to find Biff, the dog.
Then answer the questions, and follow the directions.

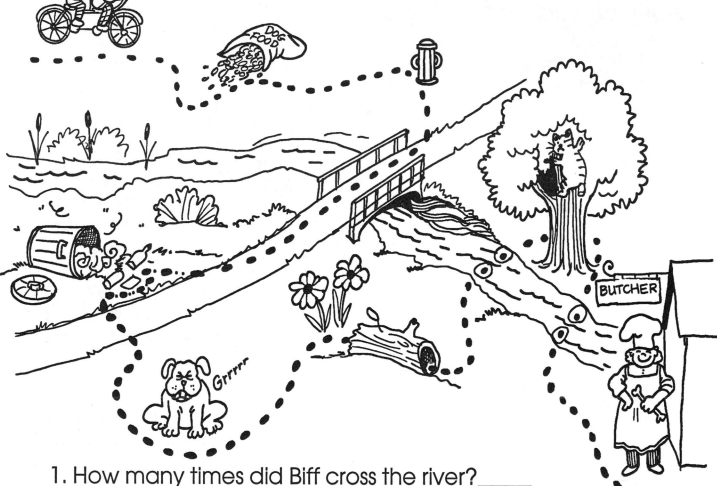

1. How many times did Biff cross the river?_____
2. Color the fire hydrant red.
3. Find the thing Biff crawled through. Color it brown.
4. Find the cat in the tree. Draw a tail on her.
5. Color the garbage can green.
6. Color the friend who gave Biff a snack.
7. Color the unfriendly dog brown.
8. Find Biff, and color the house he is in!

Name _____

Time to Celebrate!

Everybody loves a celebration! Jeff's timeline shows some events he has celebrated in his life.

Read the timeline to answer the questions.

1. What year did Jeff move to a new house? _____

2. What birthday did he celebrate in 1995? _____

3. What year did Jeff get his kitten? _____

4. What year did he learn to walk? _____

5. What year was his 4th birthday? _____

6. What year did he start school? _____

1992 Born, January 2 First tooth, May
1993 First step First word
1994 Moved to new house
1995 Third birthday New kitten named Tulip
1996 Fourth birthday Learned to ride a bike
1997 First day of school September 10th Got glasses
1998 Sixth birthday First grade New baby sister

Name _____

Read a Timeline

Social Studies Skills Test

Circle the correct answer.

1. A group of people who live together and care for each other is a

   class   shelter   family

2. Finding out new things as you grow is called

   learning   working   saving

3. Some things that tell you what you should or should not do are

   jobs   rules   wants

4. Some rules help to keep people

   safe   rich   hungry

5. A place for a person to live and keep warm and safe is a

   job   club   shelter

6. People need to work to

   stay healthy   get friends   earn money

7. Food, clothing, shelter, air, water, and love are all

   jobs   needs   goods

8. Ways people get around are called

   geography   transportation   services

Name _____

Basic Skills/Social Studies K-1

9. Which picture
   shows a need?
A  B  C

10. Which picture shows
    a want, not a need?
A B C

11. Things someone makes to sell to someone else are

        services   needs   goods

12. Texas is a   state   city   country

13. North America is a   country   continent   state

14. The United States is a   continent   state   country

15. Who is the head of the United States?

      the queen   the president   the mayor

16. Which one is a symbol
    for the United States?
A B C

17. Which continent is South America?

Name _____

Social Studies Skills Test

18. Which is a flat area of land?
mountain   lake   plain

19. Where do all people live?
on the Earth
in America
on the ocean

20. Which is true of all families around the world?
a. They all live in the same kinds of houses.
b. They all need food, clothing, shelter, air, water, and love.
c. They all eat the same kinds of food.

Draw a line to match each picture with the word that names it.

21.   island

22.

               continent

23.

               shelter

24.

               flag

25.   globe

26. Write the directions to match the picture.
Write N for north, S for south, E for east, and W for west.

a. _____
b. _____
d. _____
c. _____

Circle the correct answer.

27. The symbols on a map are
pictures   directions   words

28. A model of the Earth is called a
globe   neighborhood   state

29. The United States of America has 50
cities   mountains   states

30. George Washington was the first United States
astronaut   explorer   president

Name _____

Social Studies Skills Test

Write the correct letter and number that tell where these things are on the grid.

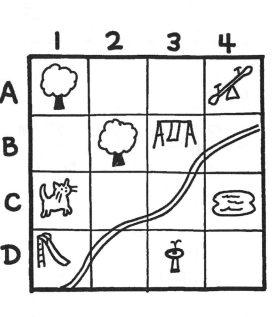

31. Where is the ? _____

32. Where is the ? _____

33. Where is the ? _____

34. Where is the ? _____

35. Where is the ? _____

Use the map at the right to answer questions 36–40.

36. How many houses are on the map? _____

37. How many stores are on the map? _____

38. Is the school on 2nd Street?
    yes   no

39. Is the lake near the hospital?
    yes   no

40. Is the airport on Main Street?
    yes   no

 house   airport

 store   hospital

 lake   school

Name _____

Social Studies Skills Test

Answer Key

Skills Test

1. family
2. learning
3. rules
4. safe
5. shelter
6. earn money
7. needs
8. transportation
9. C
10. A
11. goods
12. state
13. continent
14. country
15. the president
16. B
17. A
18. plain
19. on the Earth
20. b
21. globe
22. flag
23. island
24. continent
25. shelter
26. a. N
    b. E
    c. S
    d. W
27. pictures
28. globe
29. states
30. president
31. B, 3
32. D, 3
33. C, 1
34. D, 1
35. C, 4
36. 7
37. 5
38. no
39. yes
40. yes

Skills Exercises

pages 10-11
Answers will vary.

page 12
Answers will vary.

page 13
Answers will vary.

page 14
1. 2
2. 4
3. 1
4. 1 and 3

page 15
Answers will vary.

pages 16-17
A. 2
B. 4
C. 5
D. 4
E. 2
F. 6
G. 3
H. 7
I. 5

page 18
See that student answers fit the assignment.

page 19
See that student answers fit the assignment.

page 20
1. Layla's jobs—blue—take care of dog, clean windows
2. Dad's jobs—green—vacuum, cook dinner
3. Grandma's jobs—red—vacuum, clean windows
4. Mom's jobs—purple—wash dishes, cook dinner
5. Answers will vary.

page 21
See that student has colored an accurate person for each direction.

page 22
Answers will vary.

Copyright ©1998 by Incentive Publications, Inc., Nashville, TN.
Basic Skills/Social Studies K-1

page 23

Answers may vary somewhat.
See that student has identified at
least one appropriate example
for each word.

page 24

Real Needs: 2, 3, 6, 7, 10, 11

page 25

Answers will vary. See that student
has colored 5 things and has
circled 5 things.

pages 26–27

Match the following:
farmer on tractor—farmhouse
dog—doghouse
desert dweller on camel—tent
boy—apartment
ants—anthill
grandparents—trailer
Chinese person—Chinese-style
home
Native Americans—adobe house
bees—beehive
Eskimo—igloo
African person—grass hut

page 28

Match the following:
4—a friendship
5—a class
6—school
2—a team
1—a club
3—church

page 29

1. 4   3. 2
2. 1   4. Picture 3 should
                  be colored

pages 30–31

1. 220 Bush Street
2. The Steins
3. The Travises and the Habeebs
4. The Steins
5. Maple Street
6. 124 Maple Street

page 32

Maps will vary.

page 33

1. A, 1   4. D, 1   7. B, 3
2. C, 1   5. B, 1   8. D, 4
3. A, 3   6. D, 3

page 34

Answers will vary somewhat.
Look at pictures to see that students
have circled workers.
Possible number: 26
(Student may or may not include
biker and people in bus.)

page 35

Answers may vary. Some examples,
such as for # 7, could be explained
as either producing goods or
offering a service.
Making or growing goods,
circled red:
1, 2, 4, 7, 8, 10
Doing a service, circled blue:
3, 5, 6, 9, 11, 12
Serving Jeff and Layla:
the teacher # 12

page 36

Money cannot buy friendship
or love (# 5 and 9).

page 37

Answers will vary.

Answer Key

pages 38–39

Answers will vary. See that student has completed all exercises.

page 40

See that student has colored each of the 9 items listed.

page 41

1. Sally Ride
2. George Washington
3. Abraham Lincoln
4. Betsy Ross
5. Martin Luther King, Jr.

page 42

See that student has correctly completed the dot-to-dot.

page 43

See that student has correctly completed the dot-to-dot and has written the president's name.

pages 44–45

See that student has drawn a line from each child to the correct continent.

pages 46–47

Answers on addresses will vary. See that student has identified correct address for himself or herself.

page 48

Check to see that the items have been drawn in the correct places.

page 49

Down	Across
1. mountain	4. volcano
2. bay	5. ocean
3. globe	6. trees
	7. island

page 50

1. grass hut on stilts in rain
2. house in snow
3. desert tent
4. house with moderate climate

page 51

See that student has colored flags according to given colors.

page 52

See that student has colored flags according to given colors.

page 53

1. B, 2	5. C, 4
2. A, 4	6. A, 3
3. B, 3	7. A, 1
4. garden— green	8. clubhouse— red

page 54

See that student has written correct direction in each space, and that pictures are drawn correctly—sun in the east, sunset in the west.

page 55

See that trail the student has drawn goes from:

Jeff's apartment—Sam's house— south on Maple—swimming pool— slide—back of school— Layla's house—Maria's yard— sandbox—flagpole.

page 56

1. He crossed the river 3 times.
2–7. See that student has drawn and colored according to instructions.

page 57

1. 1994	3. 1995	5. 1996
2. 3	4. 1993	6. 1997

Copyright ©1998 by Incentive Publications, Inc., Nashville, TN.
Basic Skills/Social Studies K-1